Visions of Wanderlust

the world of travel photography

2

The very best of the past four years of the *Wanderlust* Travel Photo of the Year competition

THE MAGAZINE

Wanderlust was launched in 1993 by Paul Morrison and Lyn Hughes. It has since become the UK's leading specialist travel magazine, with its hallmark mix of inspirational writing and impartial information. Top-class photography has been a feature of the magazine from the start, aiming to show the world as it is, rather than how we might like it to be.

THE PHOTO COMPETITION

The competition is launched each July and runs to the end of the year. The panel of judges draws up a shortlist of entries, which are displayed at Destinations – the UK's leading travel and holiday show. It is here that the final judging and presentations take place. Overall winners are dispatched on a photographic commission for *Wanderlust*, recent hosts being Australia, Brazil, Japan and Kenya.

For details on entering check out the August/September, October and November issues of *Wanderlust* or log on to www.wanderlust.co.uk.

THANKS

The success of the *Wanderlust* Travel Photo of the Year competition has been due to the support of a number of individuals and organisations who share our enthusiasm for showcasing the photographic talents of our readers.

Destinations has provided the ideal venue every year for an exhibition of the finalists, and the nerve-wracking awards ceremony. Thanks to the 'Desties' team.

Our thanks must go to *The Independent*, and particularly travel editor Simon Calder, for all his encouragement and support. *The Daily Telegraph* acted as media sponsors from 2000 to 2003, so a thank you to the team there, especially Graham Boynton and Avril O'Reilly.

Our gratitude must also go out to the various sponsors over the years who have offered such excellent prizes for the competition winners, especially: Jessops, Brazil Tourism Office, Varig, Kenya Tourist Board, British Airways, Japan National Tourist Organization, All Nippon Airways, Tourism Australia, The Travel Library, Nikon and Billingham.

To the various judges and helpers, another big thanks. And last, but not least, the biggest thank you goes to all those who have entered the competition. We hope you'll feel inspired by this selection to get out there and enter again.

Contents

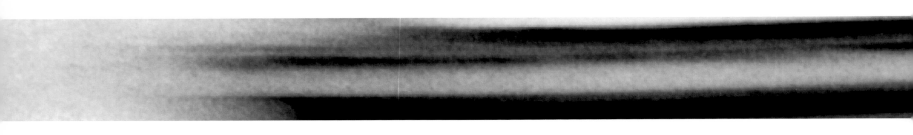

Published by Wanderlust Publications Ltd.
Leworth Place, Mellor Walk, Bachelors Acre, Windsor, SL4 1EB, UK

Tel: +44 (0)1753 620426
Fax: +44 (0)1753 620474

www.wanderlust.co.uk
Email: info@wanderlust.co.uk

Editor-in-Chief/Publisher: **Lyn Hughes**
Deputy Editor: **Piers Pickard**
Art Director: **Graham Berridge**
Sub Editors: **Sarah Baxter, Paul Bloomfield, Robert Cruse, Lizzie Matthews**
Picture Editor: **Tor McIntosh**

ISBN 0-9540926-1-9
Printed in Dubai by Emirates Printing Press.
Printed 2005.

Welcome

Welcome to the second *Visions of Wanderlust* – a showcase of some of the top entries in the *Wanderlust* Travel Photo of the Year Competition of the past four years.

In setting up the competition we wanted to capture the sense of discovery that real travellers experience on real trips. These are shots that capture a moment, rather than having been set up, and they've been taken on everything from cheap happy-snappy cameras upwards. Yet despite this, time and time again people comment on the quality, saying that they can't believe the photos haven't been taken by professionals.

The competition started in 1996 in response to the high standard of photographs that we were receiving for our regular competitions in the magazine. It rapidly became the largest travel photography competition for amateurs in the UK, culminating in a major exhibition each year at Destinations Holiday & Travel Show.

We published the first *Visions of Wanderlust* in 2001. Much has happened since then. There were no digital images included in the last book, whereas around a quarter of the images in this book were taken on digital cameras. And each year we've had the great digital debate – if a photo has been manipulated is it a true travel image? Our stunning cover shot is a manipulated image, but we have banned manipulated images from our latest competition. No doubt the debate will continue to rage.

Sadly, since the first book was published, my partner/husband/soulmate Paul Morrison has died. Paul was passionate about travel, passionate about photography, and without him there would be no *Wanderlust* Travel Photo competition and no *Visions* either. I'd like to dedicate *Visions of Wanderlust* 2 to him. I hope you get as much pleasure from the superb images in this book as he would have done.

**This book is dedicated to
Paul Morrison (1958-2004)**

LYN HUGHES, EDITOR-IN-CHIEF/PUBLISHER

1

In the Wild

Leaf tent bats, Costa Rica

"I spotted these leaf tent bats under an anthurium leaf in the Gandoca-Manzanillo refuge. They chew the veins under the leaf to make it flop over like a tent. To get this shot I had to crawl underneath without disturbing them." Danny Beath

Buachaille Etive Mór,
Glencoe, Scotland
"I had spent several mornings
trying to get this shot.
Eventually it all came
together and I was treated to
this magnificent scene."
Simon Booth

Swallow-tailed bee-eaters, Botswana
"On a morning game drive in the
Okavango I saw these bee-eaters
huddled together for warmth."
Mike Mockler

Wild dogs eating a kill,
Kruger National Park,
South Africa
Andy Skillen

Fish eagle, Lake Baringo, Kenya
"Setting off before sunrise on a small
fishing boat we spotted an eagle.
As the first rays coloured the lake,
we threw out bait and the eagle
immediately took off after it."
Dae Levy

Cheetahs, Serengeti, Tanzania
"We came across this female cheetah with
six sub-adults just as the sun was rising.
For a cheetah to raise six cubs to maturity
is extraordinary and we had a good chance
of witnessing a kill. Just an hour later
a gazelle fell victim to the mother's
hunting skill." Dae Levy

Elephant trunk and tusks,
Ngorongoro Conservation Area, Tanzania
"I persuaded the driver to wait as this bull
elephant approached – I wanted a close-up of
his massive tusks as the low setting sun
almost made them glow." James Eite

Colony of king penguins, South Georgia
"King penguins can be found on several remote island groups in the Southern Ocean and colonies are often huge – sometimes 100,000 pairs." Simon Cook

Snow leopard, Centre for Endangered Cats, Minnesota, USA
Rodney Griffiths

Lion yawning,
Masai Mara, Kenya
"Five young male lions were
sleeping under the shade of
an acacia tree after a meal
of wildebeest. I kept my
attention on one of them
and it soon rewarded
me with a wide yawn
before sleeping."
David Fletcher

Young greater flamingo,
Galápagos Islands
"I saw three flamingos fly over us in
the direction of a small lagoon so I
grabbed my bag and went running
towards them with bare feet,
stepping on some puncture vine in my
haste. The few shots of this young
flamingo were worth the pain."
Marie-Laure Stone

Monkey drinking from a tap, Zimbabwe
"At the ancient ruins of Great Zimbabwe, we
were joined by several monkeys. I set this tap
dripping and within seconds, this thirsty fellow
starting drinking." Steven Landles

Two male zebra fighting,
Kruger National Park,
South Africa
Amy Lauren Victor

Lion cub, Serengeti National Park, Tanzania
"Early one morning we came across a pride of
six females and a dozen cubs. The females
crossed a small stream and the bigger cubs
followed, leaving only the two smallest
behind. After a long hesitation they
summoned up courage and started to jump.
This one misjudged his jump and landed half
in the water." Dae Levy

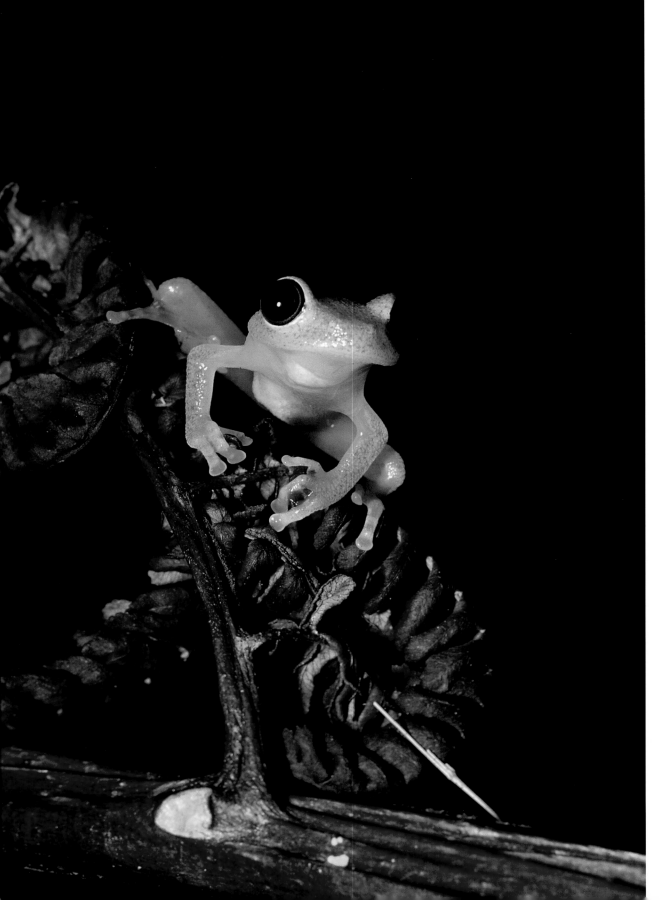

Central bright-eyed frog, Analamazaotra, Madagascar
"I took this photograph at night by a stream, using a head torch to illuminate the frog."
Graham Fenton

Lone Arctic trawler, Lofoten Islands, Norway
Bill Wastell

Lion & buffalo, Masai Mara, Kenya

"A lion/buffalo confrontation is truly a clash
of titans. This lone bull buffalo had the
misfortune to walk straight into seven male
lions hidden in the long grass. The struggle
lasted only 15 minutes." William Barr

Cheetah cubs up a tree,
Masai Mara, Kenya
"These cubs were
emulating their mother
who, unusually for a
cheetah, liked to climb
high up in acacia trees
for her 'view to a kill'."
Paul Goldstein

Pelicans, Lake Langano, Ethiopia
"I saw these four pelicans out of the corner of my eye. I had five seconds to grab my camera, turn on to AV, find them in the frame and shoot. I couldn't believe my luck when I got them, let alone sharp and in such synchronised formation."
Dominic Harcourt-Webster

Glacier at sunset, Chile
Stuart Paterson

Tree frog, Costa Rica
Danny Beath

Flamingos, Bolivia
"Laguna Colorado's colouring derives from its rich mineral content. Something startled this particular group of flamingos – fortunately I was ready and able to take a few photographs before they took flight." Nick Bellis

Early morning light,
Banff National Park,
Alberta, Canada
Lawrence Worcester

Cyclist crossing the Salar de Uyuni, Bolivia
"I was on a tour crossing Bolivia's largest salt pan in a 4WD and spotted
someone cycling to town. I grabbed my camera and fired off a few frames."
Jonathan Clay

Rannoch Moor, Scotland
John Robertson

Verreaux's sifaka, Madagascar
"This critically endangered lemur was leaping
across open grassland, making its way from
one area of forest to another."
David Nicol

Mankwe Dam at dawn,
South Africa
"At the centre of an extinct
volcano in South Africa's vast
Pilanesberg National Park
lies Mankwe Lake. It was
wreathed in mist just after dawn."
David Gurr

Canyon's glow, Arizona, USA
"Upper Antelope and Lower Antelope Canyons each contain narrow 'slot' sections carved by the occasional flash flood. Since relatively little light penetrates, the result is a cathedral-like atmosphere, in which the unbelievable red and orange colours appear to glow." Bryan Elliott

Beach on Atutaki,
Cook Islands, South Pacific
Handel Phillips

Laughing zebras, Africa

"Watching these two stallions play fighting in front of the herd, I wasted many shots trying to get them in action. Eventually, they both curled their lips up for a moment and I managed one shot – the other ones were blurred as I was laughing too." Paul Goldstein

Meerkat, Kalahari,
South Africa
"A family of meerkats was
on the move, foraging for
food after a freezing night.
This sentinel took his turn
watching for predators."
Graham Fenton

Snake swallowing a
tree frog, Tambopata
Reserve Zone,
Peruvian Amazon
Paul Franklin

Elk stag, Yellowstone
National Park, Wyoming, USA
Gloria Cotton

White pelican,
Mykonos, Greece
Martin Phillips

Cracked mud, Chile
"It rarely rains in the Atacama Desert. However, this area must have temporarily flooded in the past and then dried out, leaving the cracks. The picture talks about the past, days gone by when first the area flooded and then the fox walked through the mud." Paul Franklin

Alpine ascent, France
"This was taken from the Aiguille de Midi, Chamonix, the highest cable car in Europe, at 3,350m. The air was clear, as was the view."
Ron Tear

Royal terns mating, Sanibel Island, Florida, USA
"These terns were from a medium-sized colony at the start of their mating season.
With a little patience and persistence I was able to isolate a pair during courtship." Simon Booth

2
Work & Play

Man sorting tomatoes, Azrou, Morocco
"Just after dawn, the early morning light brings out the best of the colours of the produce." Ian Gardener

Walking on Glacier Grey,
Chile
"At night in the Torres del
Paine NP, huge chunks of
ice could be heard
crashing into the lake
from where we were
camped." Alan Dykes

Car mechanics, Cameroon

"Exploring a visually rich but less desirable area of Yaoundé, the capital of Cameroon, I was warned that it might not be safe for photography. However, some amenable car mechanics made interesting subjects and a little beer money delighted them." Martin Philips

Monk & water spray, Laos
"On our way through Luang Prabang we passed a wat where a young monk was beating a skin drum dry. He was clearly enjoying his work." Keith Harris

Motorcyclist in the Gobi Desert, Mongolia
"Travelling from Ulaanbaatar to the Gobi Desert, I saw this biker approaching, a dark shimmer in the distance, taking what seemed like a lifetime to reach us. We both stopped, as is common courtesy on a lonely road, and greeted one another."
Beth Woollam

Pigs in transit, Vietnam
"My motorbike driver and I had stopped on the side of the road when I saw these two locals and their pigs go past. I jumped up and tried to tell my driver that I wanted to catch them. After much miming he finally understood and we sped off in hot pursuit."
Damian Prestidge

Street workers,
Rio de Janeiro, Brazil
"I noticed these workers one
morning when I was looking
down from the balcony of
our hotel overlooking
Ipanema Beach." Victoria Fry

Mikoshi mayhem,
Tokyo, Japan
"*Mikoshi* festivals are
crazy events when
ordinary men and women
put on a short kimono,
drink too much and carry
the incredibly heavy
mikoshi (portable shrines)
around the streets. The
whole thing is utter chaos,
with an energy that makes
a modern city such as
Tokyo seem like a totally
different, more rustic,
more Asian place
altogether."
Damon Coulter

Beach kids at Sihanoukville, Cambodia
"These children live, work and play on the beaches all day, skipping
school to make money from the tourists by selling fruit and making
bracelets. I was glad to capture a moment of their play time during
a game of football in the afternoon sun." Jon Tonks

3
Town & Country

Shaka's Rock, South Africa

"This photo was taken overlooking the lovely Thompson's Bay, near Durban. I had risen at 4am to get the photo and relied on a lot of good fortune as I'd never tried slow shutter exposures – I needed the weather to play its part." Alec Turner

Beached ship, Beira, Mozambique

"On a walk late one afternoon I came across this amazing sight. The size of the boat was
phenomenal and it looked as if it could fall over at any time." Steven Landles

Grand Summons, China

"In the presence of the Living Buddha, monks attend a debate during the Grand Summons of the Labrang Monastery, Xiahe, Gansu Province." Jeremy Hunter

Seattle, Washington, USA

Michael Surowiak

Flapping chicken, Chiang Saen, northern Thailand
"This prized teahouse chicken was greeting the dawn beside the Mekong River. His owner was confused but pleased that I spent so much time photographing it."
Lawrence Worcester

Buddhist monks outside an internet café, Phnom Penh, Cambodia
"Every morning the monks do their rounds to collect alms. I saw these and thought that the juxtaposition of a practice that has been going on for centuries with all the logos of the cyber age was too good to miss."
Edward Sheen

San Cristóbal, Mexico
"This photo sums up everything about Mexico – the elegant decay of buildings, the ubiquitous VW Beetle, the ice-cream seller, the guard with the machine gun and, most of all, the heat. I had to stand in the way of moving traffic to get this one, but I think it was worth it."
Will Rolls

San Francisco, USA
"Union Square is photographed a lot, but I got a different view when I visited Macy's department store on the far side. I got out on to the roof and shot this through the 'a' of the metal lettering of 'Macy's.'" Will Rolls

Catedral de NS do Pilar reflected in car bonnet,
São João del Rei, Brazil
John Pennock

Kumbh bridges, Allahabad, India
"These were just some of the bridges that had
been built for the Kumbh Mela, the largest
religious festival in the world. Over 100 million
people would attend the gathering over the
coming weeks." Colin Hutton

Boatman in front
of the Taj Mahal,
Agra, India
Kim Van

Wig stall, Ghana
"This wig stand was photographed
in Hohoe, a small town in the east
of the country." Jill Jones

Spot the dog, Trinidad, Cuba
"I was photographing an interesting doorway and couldn't believe my luck when 'Spot' suddenly pushed his way out from behind the bright blue frame."
Mavis Roper

Boat framed by rock arch,
Algarve, Portugal
Martin Phillips

Traditional hat by a stream in the altiplano, Bolivia
"We stopped at this fantastic stream for lunch. While wandering around I spotted our Bolivian guide's wife's hat, left by the bank. I grabbed a couple of shots before she spotted me, laughed and popped it back on her head."
Nicky Van der Bij

Etna erupting, Sicily
"A few moments after taking this image, a hither-to-hidden vent cleared its throat. Several bombs thudded into the ground beyond us at high speed – but not as fast as our 'grab everything and run' retreat about a second later. It was a good day."
Jeremy Bishop

Jodhpur, Rajasthan, India
"Houses in Jodhpur are painted
blue to indicate that the residents
are Brahmins." Lucy Stewart

Independence Day celebrations, St Louis, USA

"As I stood in front of the old courthouse, the sky erupted into a blaze of colour and noise. It was like being in World War III for at least half an hour." Danny Beath

Remarkable rocks,
Flinders Chase National Park,
Kangaroo Island, South Australia
Janet Edwards

Block of flats, Hanoi, Vietnam
"This is a showcase of everyday
life in Vietnam's capital.
Doors and windows are painted
colourfully, matching the garnish
of laundry and curtains peeping
from opened windows."
Mike Yamanouchi

Fishermen on the Nile near Luxor, Egypt

"I noticed the fishermen on the felucca quietly going about their business, oblivious to the splendour of the scene."
Colin Atkinson

Copacabana Beach, Rio de Janeiro, Brazil

"These vendors sell thick sweet bread or cake, all day long.
This quick-grab shot, with Ipanema Point in the distance
and a jogger about to cross the road, seemed perfect."
Justin Wastnage

Three monks crossing bridge, Inle Lake, Shan State, Burma (Myanmar)
"I awoke at 5am and came across these three monks crossing the bridge. The subject, cool air and filtered morning light resulted in an image that is both haunting and an inspiration to many early mornings since." Cameron Hansen

**Prayer wheels,
Kathmandu, Nepal**
Dr Tejas Udani

**Rickshaw in
Calcutta, India**
"This rickshaw
puller was
photographed in
the commercial
sector of Calcutta
during the
monsoon season."
Amvrosios Demou

Tower Bridge,
London, UK
Billy Stock

Gondolas, Venice, Italy
"Standing on Saint Mark's Square I was planning a shot of the gondolas from an interesting angle when a boat went past – the resulting wake caused a few waves to hit the side." Tim Molema

Morning crowds at Grand Central Station, New York, USA
"I went out specifically to capture the rush hour. The bonus of the morning sun shining through the windows really made the picture."
Ian Yates

Boatman, River Ganges, Varanasi, India

"The early-morning mist had almost lifted and the sun starting to shine through as
I took this shot, using a very wide-angle lens to capture the boatman, his boat and
the surroundings." Alan Fretten

Nash Point,
Vale of Glamorgan,
Wales
Billy Stock

4

Face to Face

Young monk, Phnom Penh, Cambodia

"I saw this young monk at school at Wat Saravoan, daydreaming during a maths lesson." Andy Sewell

Young girl, Kathmandu, Nepal
"On a rainy September morning,
this girl and I both sheltered from
the weather." Marco Pozzi

San woman, Kalahari Desert,
Botswana
"Xhanakadie is a San elder (or
Bushwoman), resting after
Independence Day celebrations
in Botswana." Amanda Gazidis

Smiling woman,
Jaisalmer, India
"She raised her arm to
cover her face, but she
was smiling and
obviously flattered. I
hope the photograph
captures a little of
her personality."
Nigel Nagarajan

Sisters of the *sukumbasi*, Pokhara, Nepal
"The girls stood outside their one-roomed home in the *sukumbasi* (slums) of Pokhara, eating traditional *dhal bhat* (rice, lentils and curried vegetables)."
Sharon Oliver

Village tribespeople, Rajasthan, India
"Akoda village lies with five other tiny tribal settlements north of Bundi, far off the beaten track. The people were happy, extremely friendly and sometimes very shy."
Paul Exton

Holy hand, Varanasi, India
"This holy man was preparing to go to the Kumbh Mela, a festival that takes place every three years. When asked if I could take his picture he raised his hand up – not to stop me, but because he wanted me to see it."
Colin Hutton

H'mong girl, Sapa, Vietnam
"I met this girl in the hills of northern
Vietnam, on the Chinese border. She
agreed that I could take her picture if
I bought one of her home-made hats –
she was a strong business woman."
Ian Longthorne

Reclining girl from
Padaung hilltribe,
Nai Soi village,
Mae Hong Son province,
northern Thailand
"Due to hordes of
tourists taking their
photo, the Padaung tribe
have become stiff in their
posing ways. I sat and
talked to them for half an
hour until this Padaung
girl was completely
comfortable in
my presence."
Simon Spicknell

Zebra, Hwange National Park, Zimbabwe
"This magnificent zebra met us on the bush track near Nyamandhlovu platform. We seemed to have an equal fascination for each other."
Liz Kingston

Old woman, Hoi An, Vietnam
"My wife and I had been sitting with this lady while she prepared food. I can't recall what my wife did to make her laugh, but the result was this very natural expression (or a dentist's nightmare)." Alan Fretten

Samburu women at a village market, northern Kenya
"We were stranded for several hours when our expedition truck stopped to make repairs and, as always happens on such occasions, a group of locals gathered to watch. These calm, beautiful women were a photographer's gift."
John Dinham

Himba woman, Namibia
Gloria Cotton

Miner in Cerro Rico (Rich Hill), Potosí, Bolivia
"This miner was extracting tin ore using only a hammer and a carbide lamp. He is chewing coca leaves (the reason his mouth is black), which suppress appetite and fatigue, enabling the miners to work long hours with little food."
Paul Franklin

Turkana tribeswoman, Kenya

"I took this photo on the shores of Lake Turkana, often called the Jade Sea. Sadly the beautiful customs and traditions of Kenya's tribal peoples are dying out." Louisa Seton

Smoking man with son from
Kreung hilltribe, Nanglet
village, Ratanakiri province,
Cambodia
"Cambodia has over 30
different ethnic groups but,
unlike neighbouring
countries, its minorities do
not wear colourful attire
and are quite
hard to distinguish
from the Khmer people."
Simon Spicknell

Tibetan traders with
transistor radio,
Namche Bazaar, Nepal
Dawn Edmonds

Vine snake,
Western Ghats, India
DK Bhaskar

Two monkeys admire an ancient Buddha carving, Lopburi, Thailand
Lawrence Worcester

Blue-footed boobies, Isla de la Plata, Ecuador
Jonathan Clay

Hiding boy, Ecuador
"We were travelling through the central sierra, riding on the roof of El Nariz del Diablo (The Devil's Nose) train from Riobamba. As this young boy passed me on the platform, he stole this look back at me as he hid behind his mother's brightly coloured poncho."
Nick Harper

Short-sighted shepherd,
Rajasthan, India
"I came across this lovely
character up in the hills,
outside Udaipur. He happily
let me take his photograph
as he walked home from the
fields." Minky Sloane

Tibetan woman with a
Buddhist prayer wheel,
Lhasa, Tibet
"A magical display of
devotion." Natalia Cohen

Orphan playing bamboo pipes, Indonesia
"This picture was taken at an orphanage near Rantepao, Tana Toraja. A group of youngsters
were assembled to play a variety of bamboo musical instruments, ably conducted by one of their own."
Christopher Marsham

Maori dancer, Te Papa
(National Museum),
Wellington, New Zealand
"This group performed a
traditional dance at the
opening of a new
exhibition about the
Tühoe people."
Andy Sewell

Smiling woman, Ghana
"Intrigued by her lovely
face, warmth and
modesty, I asked
this lady for permission
to photograph her. She
asked: 'Why do you want
to photograph me?' to
which I replied: 'Because
you look beautiful!'"
Elsbeth Linnhoff

Rothschild's giraffe,
Giraffe Centre,
near Nairobi, Kenya
"The Leslie-Melville family
created the African Fund for
Endangered Wildlife to save this
sub-species from extinction.
From a count of 130 in the 1970s,
there are now some 350 in safe
areas." John Merrills

Mantis, Mount Isa,
Queensland, Australia
Graham Reardon

Armed Mursi woman,
Omo Valley,
western Ethiopia
"The Mursi's relations
with neighbouring tribes
are characterised by
periods of war and peace.
The introduction of
modern weapons and
irregular rains has
aggravated conflicts
since the 1970s."
Antony Penney

Quechua boy, Peru
"This photo was shot in the Peruvian Andes. I was living in a village for a month which gave me the opportunity to get to know the normally shy local people quite well. The boy is wearing the poncho and hat that is traditional in that region." Paul Franklin

Biker, Tombstone, Arizona, USA
Mike Kirk

Man and camel, Egypt
"His camel just put its
head on his shoulder
and closed its eyes in
that dreamy way –
it looked so content!"
Dr Celia Mannings

Camel and camelman,
Jaisalmer, India
"This camelman's intriguing face caught my eye – his turban looked almost luminous in the warm light. When he agreed to have his photo taken, the camel was determined not to be left out of the shot."
Lynne McIntosh

Eagle hunter, Mongolia
"Several years ago, *Wanderlust* published a picture of an eagle hunter in Mongolia, which inspired me to travel there myself." Tanya Millard

Woman smoking a cigar, Burma (Myanmar)
"Wandering around a market on the shores
of Inle Lake, I stopped to chat and take shots
of some of the lovely women sitting around
eating and smoking cheroots." Jackie Ellis

Old peasant, Yangshuo,
Guangxi, China
"We rented bikes and came across
this frail old man in the paddy fields
in Yangshuo. He had cataracts, could
only breathe through his mouth,
and was so old he could not
remember his age."
Marie-Laure Stone

Plains Indian hoop dancer,
Calgary Stampede,
Alberta, Canada
John Colmer

5
Digital

Green turtle, Bora Bora, French Polynesia Chris Lambert

Mr & Mrs
Boonmalart,
Bangkok, Thailand
Lynn Frieda

Toucan, Iguaçu Falls NP, Brazil/Argentina border
"I was drawn to this shot by the iridescent blue of
the toucan's eye." Graeme Dougan

Christmas in New York, USA
Mark Doherty

Dhoni at anchor, the Maldives
"This was taken while snorkelling, and I planned to take advantage of a calm sea and shoaling fish. The image was taken in two halves and blended digitally."
Penny Piddock

Monk crossing the U Beins Bridge at sunset, Burma (Myanmar)
"Sunset is a busy time for locals and visitors alike at the world's longest teak bridge. But for the briefest moment the bicycles and beanie hats were gone as a lone monk crossed during the last few seconds of the setting sun."
Paul Strawson

Exodus at sunset, Aït Benhaddou, Morocco
"I was taken aback by the striking scene at sunset, and had to run back down ahead of the group to capture this striking shot before everyone descended." Jill Templeton

The Pinnacles, Western Australia
"Thousands of limestone spires – the fossilised roots of long-dead trees – varying from truck-sized six-metre giants to finger-thick pieces of piping: the Pinnacles have to be seen to be believed."
Laurie Wilson

Greenwich foot tunnel, London

"Taken on a stormy night in heavy rain, the reflections from the wet ground brought out the colour and pattern of the foreground, while the clouds were low enough to reflect the lights from Canary Wharf." John Pennock

Blue tranquillity, Greece

"The monastery of Vlakherna is said to have been Odysseus' ship, turned to stone by the sea god Poseidon." Graeme Stuart Pollock

Zebra at midnight,
Kilaguni Lodge,
Tsavo West National
Park, Kenya
"There was just enough
light to see the zebras
but barely enough for
photography. For a few
shots the animals obliged,
staying still long enough
to get a usable image."
Penny Piddock

Girl with water jar,
Inle Lake, Burma (Myanmar)
Christian Kober

Day gecko, northern Madagascar
"This gecko was so engrossed in lunch that it hardly noticed the camera lens as I got up close to capture the detail." Jill Templeton

Horseman & horses on Pink Sands Beach, Harbour Island, Bahamas

"For Marty the horseman, the hurricane season meant a two-month slump in business. He used this time to take his horses down to the beach and into the sea to cool off." Sandra Hunter

Bears fighting, Knight Inlet, British Columbia, Canada

"While photographing grizzly bears feeding on the spawning salmon, angry growls erupted behind us.
Two 225kg bears were facing each other, cuffing and biting, water spraying everywhere." Marie-Laure Stone

Don't walk, San Francisco, USA
"Lights were just coming on in the buildings and street, and the dusk light accentuated the impact of the 'Don't Walk' sign. I risked life and limb by stepping into the road during a gap in the traffic to grab a quick shot."
Stephen Eeley

The Forbidden City, Beijing
"The day before, it had started to snow quite heavily – nearly paralysing Beijing's traffic. The bright blue skies and freshly fallen snow made the Forbidden City look all the more impressive." Fred Chan

Pushkar Camel Fair, Rajasthan, India
Paul Strawson

Man praying by the Ganges, India
"The ghats (steps) are the spiritual centre of Varanasi, allowing access to the holy River Ganges." Marco Pozzi

Portrait of a marriage, Otavalo, Ecuador
"I thought that the appearance of these characters depicted very well not only their ethnic and cultural background but also the hardness of their lives." Marco Pozzi

Aurora borealis,
Tysfjord, Norway
Lee Hiom

Buddhist nun smoking a cheroot,
Mingun, Burma (Myanmar)
"The cheroot was a somewhat unusual
donation – we're not sure if the giver would
gain merit – but the nun seemed to be
appreciating it." Paul Strawson

Children laughing, Sulawesi, Indonesia
"I heard a young Bajau calling 'Photo saya!', which
translates as 'picture me'. The child began
scrambling up a post in an effort to catch my
attention." Sylvia Munday

The Göreme Valley of Cappadocia, Turkey
"Over the centuries, wind and erosion have
created formations called 'fairy chimneys'
in the tuff of the once-volcanic area
of Cappadocia." Charles Cotton

Dung beetle,
Shamwari Game
Reserve, South Africa
Louise Drew

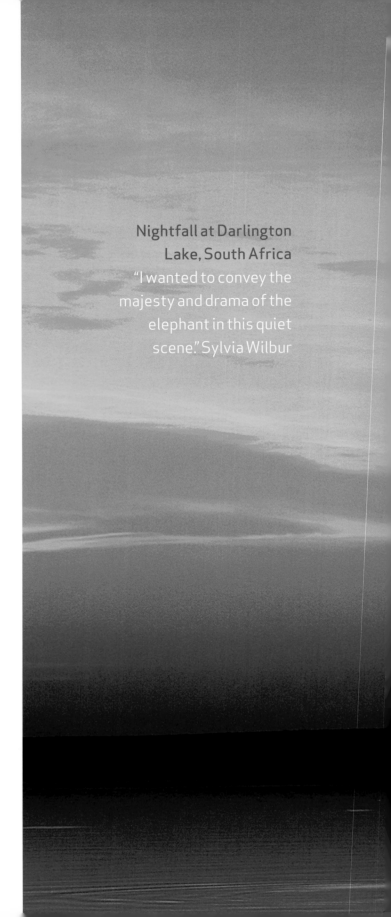

Nightfall at Darlington
Lake, South Africa
"I wanted to convey the
majesty and drama of the
elephant in this quiet
scene." Sylvia Wilbur

Sally Lightfoot crab, Galápagos Islands, Ecuador

"Most of the wildlife in the Galápagos is relatively unafraid of people– it doesn't see humans as predators but more as passing curiosities that come and stare every now and then."

Andrew Chong